AMERICAN IMPRESSIONISTS

AMERICAN IMPRESSIONISTS

Elizabeth Miles Montgomery

Crescent Books
New York

Page 1:

FRANK BENSON

The Hilltop
1903, oil on canvas, 71 × 51 in.
Malden Public Library, Malden, MA

Page 2:

WILLIAM MERRITT CHASE

Self-Portrait (Portrait of the Artist)
1915-16, oil on canvas, 52½ × 63 in.
Art Association of Richmond, Richmond, IN

Pages 4-5:

WILLIAM MERRITT CHASE

The Cloisters
1888, oil on canvas, 14⅝ × 27⅝ in.
Gift of Mrs. Frank Tillar,
The Arkansas Arts Center Foundation, Little Rock, AK

This 1991 edition published by Crescent Books,
distributed by Outlet Book Company, Inc.,
a Random House Company,
225 Park Avenue South,
New York, New York 10003

Produced by
Brompton Books Corporation
15 Sherwood Place,
Greenwich, CT 06830

ISBN 0-517-06514-2

8 7 6 5 4 3 2 1

Printed and bound in Hong Kong

CONTENTS

INTRODUCTION

The artistic movement known as Impressionism was first identified in 1874 when a group of French artists, dissatisfied with the reception of their works by the academic art establishment of the period, chose to hold a separate exhibition of their paintings. The movement received its name when critic Louis Leroy used the term Impressionism – no doubt he was inspired by Claude Monet's *Impression: Sunrise* – in his scathing review of the entire group.

Despite obvious differences in style, all of these painters were connected by an ability to catch a moment and preserve it on canvas, and in their belief in the importance of that moment. They readily accepted and made use of the technological advances available to them, and in the end became recognized as proponents of one of the most significant movements in the history of art.

The movement produced an aesthetic revolution in art, and as with many radical ideas, it was greeted with dismay and dislike. The changes Impressionism made paved the way for more radical styles. Because of the rapid succession of new movements – from Futurism and Surrealism to Abstract Art –

American Impressionism quickly fell out of favor. But for a decade or so around the turn of the century, Impressionism was the mainstream style in American painting.

The American Impressionists had the advantage of following in the footsteps of their French counterparts in a climate of artistic appreciation in the United States that was less entrenched in conventions and therefore more receptive to Impressionism. In the United States the art establishment was not as powerful as it was on the Continent. The idea of art of any kind was still somewhat radical, and the conventions of art were much looser. Several different styles of painting became acceptable at the same time, so that artists as diverse as Thomas Eakins, Winslow Homer, and Frederic Church all had adherents in the late 1880s. It was Homer who came closest to the Impressionist style, but his choice of subject matter, his palette, and his technique mark him as unique.

The work of some French Impressionists was seen in the United States even before 1886, the year when the well-known French art dealer, Paul Durand-Ruel, mounted an exhibition of 300 paintings by such artists as Monet, Edouard Manet,

Left: Artists on the back porch, Griswold House, Old Lyme, CT, c. 1903.

Right: Winslow Homer's *Sunlight and Shadow,* painted in 1872.

Pierre-Auguste Renoir, and Edgar Degas. In contrast to the first Impressionist exhibition in Paris in 1874, this one was a triumph. Durand-Ruel wrote, "[it] was an immense success, for reasons of curiosity, but as opposed to what happened in Paris, it provoked neither uproar, nor abusive comment, arousing no protest whatsoever. The general public as well as every amateur came, not to laugh, but to learn about these notorious paintings which caused such a stir in Paris."

It is evident from Durand-Ruel that there was already great interest and knowledge of the French Impressionists in the United States at a time when they were still ignored and reviled in their own country. Certain collectors, such as Mr. and Mrs. H.O. Havemeyer and Alexander Cassatt, had been buying French Impressionist paintings for several years, and were in a position to lend some notable works to Durand-Ruel for his exhibition. This exhibit was moved after a month to the National Academy of Design, and the duration of the exhibition was extended because so many people wanted to see it.

Many Americans went abroad to study at the various academies and ateliers, and became conversant with the latest techniques and styles. Mary Cassatt, the first major American Impressionist, had been traveling to Europe and studying painting since she was a child. In 1871, after finding little interest in her work in the United States, she returned to Europe, eventually arriving back in Paris where she was confronted by the changes in art that had taken place since her last visit. "How well I

remember," she wrote years later to her friend and art collector Louisine Havemeyer, "seeing for the first time Degas' pastels in the window of a picture dealer on the Boulevard Haussmann. I used to go and flatten my nose against that window and absorb all I could of his art. It changed my life. I saw art then as I wanted to see it."

Some of what Cassatt saw she began to incorporate into her own work. Though her work had been accepted and exhibited with the Salon, she was invited to join the Impressionists by Degas. In 1879 she finally submitted one of the paintings that marks her most clearly as a member of the movement. This was a portrait of her sister, now known as *Woman with a Pearl Necklace in a Loge*. At that time, the American reviewers' opinions were consistent with those of their French brethren, and the criticism leveled at this work was harsh indeed. A critic from *The New York Times* wrote, "I am sorry for Mary Cassatt; she is a Philadelphian, and has had her place in the Salon – a great triumph for a woman and a foreigner; but why has she gone thus astray! Her *Lady in an Opera-box* is a nasty representation of a dirty-faced female, in variegated raiment, who in real life, would never have been admitted in decent society until she washed her face and shoulders, while the background looks as though it was painted with the yolk of an egg." *Lydia in a Loge* is, perhaps, the first painting by an American in the Impressionist style to be included and reviewed by the American press.

Mary Cassatt was not the only American to work with the French Impressionists, and to learn from them. Through the Impressionists, Americans studying abroad learned about Japanese art, which was to become a major influence on Impressionism. For centuries Japan had been closed to outside influences. The artists of the West had been fascinated by the exotic East for centuries. This fascination had manifested itself in the pseudo-Egyptian motifs of Napoleonic France, the Arabic paintings of Delacroix, and in the collecting of porcelain, among others. When the American Commodore Matthew C. Perry anchored his ships in lower Tokyo Bay and negotiated a treaty in 1854, he opened the eyes of the world to centuries of Japanese culture. One result of this was that the Impressionists and other artists began to study and collect various kinds of Japanese art. They seemed most fascinated by the woodblock prints, and some of this influence was reflected in their own work. Mary Cassatt did a series of etchings in the 1890s that successfully combined the Japanese style and sophisticated sense of color with a Western subject. James Abbott McNeill Whistler was among the first artists to collect Eastern art and to adapt the Japanese sense of composition to his own work.

Artists of the period also delighted in collecting Oriental artifacts to use in their paintings. The kimono-clad model standing or seated in front of an oriental screen almost became a cliche. And many of the garden paintings were enhanced by the inclusion of a paper parasol.

Technological innovations were also a major influence on the rise of Impressionism. One of the new advances was photography, whose beginnings date back to the invention of the

Left: Mary Cassatt submitted her *Woman with a Pearl Necklace in a Loge* for an Impressionist exhibition in 1879.

Right: James McNeill Whistler's passion for all things oriental is presented here in his *The Princess from the Land of Porcelain.*

Left: Members of an artists' colony in Cos Cob, Connecticut, show the dramatic impact Japanese culture had on them by having a tea ceremony in Far Eastern dress.

daguerreotype in 1839. Some artists declared that the new invention would be the death of painting and would have nothing to do with it. Others found it a useful tool. One of those was Theodore Robinson, an American who worked at Giverny – where he was befriended by Monet – during his last years in France. "The camera," wrote Robinson, "helps retain the picture in your mind." It also allowed painters to dispense with long, tiring sittings by models, under certain circumstances. These painters never copied the photographs exactly, despite certain criticisms that accused them of doing so.

Several other technological breakthroughs were responsible, to some degree, for the creation and execution of the new Impressionist style. One of these was the invention of the metal ferrule which held bristles flat. This brush gave the painter greater control and enabled him to make the characteristic flat strokes. Another useful invention was the collapsible tin tube. This easily reclosed container preserved the oil paint in a stable condition without changing the color. It was a great improvement over animal bladders, which had been used to hold oil paint – after it had been specially ground – since the days of the Renaissance masters. The new tube was portable and made it possible for artists to work outside, or *en plein-air*. This freedom made possible many of the Impressionist paintings with the feeling of immediacy or "catching the moment."

Another innovation was color. Nineteenth-century chemists created a new palette of colors, derived from coal tar and other substances. These were first used by fabric manufacturers, and then adopted by painters. They include some of the brighter colors, including cobalt blue, emerald green, and chrome yellow, whose tones give the Impressionist paintings their characteristic shimmering quality.

Most but not all of these technological innovations had been available to the painters of the Barbizon School. The Barbizon, which preceded the Impressionists, explored the forces of nature and was concerned with the light and atmosphere of each scene. The most important technical difference between the Impressionists and the Barbizon School was one of color. The Impressionists did away with the murky shadows of the Barbizon and used vibrant new colors in their place. The Impressionists turned from a stable permanent world to one of immediacy and movement. They also rejected the anecdotal subjects that had been popular for so long in favor of scenes of everyday life. Though it seems a natural progression today, this new way of painting demanded a new way of seeing. The painters of the Impressionist school understood the study of optics and used their knowledge to place complementary colors side by side on the canvas and let the eye mix them, rather than mixing them on the palette. It was this radical use of color that challenged all the old rules that had been established and held in regard for so long.

The World Columbian Exposition of 1893 was held only seven years after the Durand-Ruel exhibit. The American entries in the art gallery totaled 2395, most of which showed French influences. In his book *Crumbling Idols*, Hamlin Garland wrote: "If the Exposition had been held five years ago, scarcely a trace of the blue shadow idea would have been seen outside the work of Claude Monet, Pissarro and a few others of the French and Spanish groups." Most of the painters now considered American Impressionists exhibited – showing etchings and watercolors, as well as oils. Mary Cassatt even painted some of the murals in the Women's Building. It became obvious that the new style had traveled across the ocean.

One reason why the techniques and styles of the French Impressionists were coming to America was that many of those

The photographic study Theodore Robinson used for his work *Two in a Boat.*

Robinson's *Two in a Boat.* Note that Robinson did not merely copy the photograph; the tree branch and a third boat have been left out of his composition.

artists who had studied in Europe returned to the United States to teach in the art schools that had begun to spring up all over the United States. The first American art school had been the Pennsylvania Academy of Fine Arts, founded in Philadelphia in 1806. Other schools such as the American Academy of Arts in New York, chartered in 1808, and the National Academy of Design, chartered in 1825, followed. By the 1890s, there were art schools from Boston to California, and at least one faculty member in each had probably been to France and studied with the Impressionists. Robert Vonnoh was one such student who had studied with the Impressionists, and had attended the

Académie Julian in Paris. He returned to America to teach at the Pennsylvania Academy of Fine Arts. His pupils, who all tried painting in the Impressionist style, included Robert Henri, William Glackens, John Sloan, and Maxfield Parrish.

Other artists began to establish summer schools and art colonies where they could instruct and work with congenial company in a picturesque setting. The artists working along the Connecticut shore, such as Willard Metcalf, Childe Hassam, and John Twachtman, began to create a body of work done in a single place, which would make those American places almost as recognizable as the gardens and haystacks of Giverny.

In December 1897, after much discussion, eleven painters resigned from the Society of American Artists. These painters – Julian Alden Weir, John Twachtman, Childe Hassam, Willard Metcalf, Thomas Dewing, Edmund Tarbell, Frank Benson, Robert Reid, Joseph De Camp, E.E. Simmons, and Abbott Thayer – formed their own association and mounted their own exhibition the following spring. According to *The New York Times*, "It is not the intention of these gentlemen to organize a rival society, or indeed to form an organization at all, Mr. Weir said last evening. He said that the seceding artists grew dissatisfied with their membership in a large body which was governed by form and tradition, and having sympathetic tastes in a certain direction in art, they had withdrawn from the Society of American Artists to work together in accordance with those tastes. Mr. Weir said that one object of his friends and himself following the Japanese view, is to get rid of the barbaric idea of large exhibitions of paintings, and so they propose to give each year a small exhibition limited to the best three or four paintings of the men interested in the new movement."

They held their first exhibition in the spring of 1898. By that time, Abbott Thayer, who is best known for his paintings of idealized women and quasi-religious winged figures, had backed out. They had also asked Winslow Homer to join, but the artist, who was a good ten years older than any of the others, declined, although he wrote expressing support and even a certain amount of envy for their plans for exhibitions.

Years later, another member of the group, Edward Simmons, would recall, "We were just a group who wanted to make a showing and left the Society as a protest against big exhibits.

At our first exhibition at the Durand-Ruel's Gallery we merely put out the sign – 'Show of Ten American Painters' – and it was the reporters and critics speaking of us who gave us the name [the Ten]. In the original group were Twachtman, Dewing, Metcalf, Reid, Hassam, Weir, Benson, De Camp, Tarbell and myself. After the death of Twachtman, Chase was voted to take his place . . . . The first few years we divided the wall into equal spaces and drew lots for them, each man having the right to use it as he saw fit, hanging one picture or a number of pictures . . ."

The exhibition was a success, and remained an annual feature of the New York art scene until 1918. The small size of the show, which usually numbered about forty works of art, did not require the stamina and effort that was necessary to view the vast number of paintings hung in tiers at the Academy and Society exhibitions. The new "Japanese" form of installation, or hanging paintings on a single line, added to the ease of viewing. The painters even went as far as changing the color of the walls in the gallery if another tone would provide a better background for their pictures. It was a method they had picked up from Whistler, who had also favored hanging pictures on a line.

The critics were somewhat surprised that the rebellious artists were not experimenting with new art forms. The group merely practiced variations of the French Impressionist style, and the fact that the critics did not find this radical is proof enough that the style had been accepted at least in the United States by 1898, only twelve years after Durand-Ruel's first exhibition.

There were, of course, variations within the style, and none of the Ten painted in exactly the same way. Childe Hassam, one of the founders and most successful members of the group, is, after Mary Cassatt, the artist most closely associated with the French Impressionists. Born in Dorchester, Massachusetts, in 1859, he studied in Boston and abroad. Hassam settled in Paris in 1886 and attended classes at the Académie Julian. His early works, especially his paintings of the streets of Paris and Boston, are very tonal. At the Paris Salon in 1887 he exhibited *Grand-Prix Day*. Created with quick brush strokes, it is a colorful, sunlight painting of the equipages on the Champs-Elysees. It won Hassam a gold medal. He returned to the United States after winning a bronze medal at the Exposition Universelle in 1889, and established a studio in New York. During the summer, he traveled in New England, staying on the Isles of Shoals for several summers, where he taught the poet Celia Thaxter. Hassam later immortalized her garden at Appledore. After her death in 1894, he joined the summer colony in Cos Cob, Connecticut, and also painted in Old Lyme, Connecticut, for several years, enjoying the change of light. He continued to paint cityscapes, and may be best known for the series of flag pictures that combine buildings, moving flags, and crowds. His later work has hints of Post-Impressionism, but he basically remained an Impressionist long after the style had fallen out of favor.

Left: The Ten in 1908. Bottom row (l-r): E.E. Simmons, Willard Metcalf, Childe Hassam, J. Alden Weir, Robert Reid; top row (l-r): William Merritt Chase, Frank Benson, Edmund Tarbell, Thomas Dewing, Joseph De Camp.

Right: Hassam's *The Etcher: Self-Portrait.* An accomplished printmaker, Hassam was the American whose work came closest to Monet's, though he never went to Giverny.

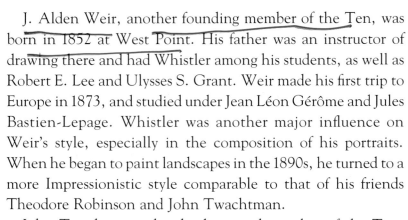

J. Alden Weir, another founding member of the Ten, was born in 1852 at West Point. His father was an instructor of drawing there and had Whistler among his students, as well as Robert E. Lee and Ulysses S. Grant. Weir made his first trip to Europe in 1873, and studied under Jean Léon Gérôme and Jules Bastien-Lepage. Whistler was another major influence on Weir's style, especially in the composition of his portraits. When he began to paint landscapes in the 1890s, he turned to a more Impressionistic style comparable to that of his friends Theodore Robinson and John Twachtman.

John Twachtman, the third original member of the Ten, studied art with Frank Duveneck in Cincinnati, the city of his birth. He went to Munich with Duveneck and William Merritt Chase in 1875, when he was twenty-two. Admitted to the Society of American Artists in 1879, he returned to Europe to teach at Duveneck's school in Florence. It was probably at this time that he met Whistler. After his marriage in 1883, he and his wife moved to Paris where Twachtman studied at the Académie Julian, and painted cool, misty landscapes in the manner of Japanese prints. The following years marked his greatest popularity as a painter, and he was able to buy a farm in Greenwich, Connecticut. His farm became the subject of many of his later works, which were increasingly abstract. These abstractions were misunderstood by the public and his later works did not sell well at all. He died, embittered, in 1902.

The artist of the Ten whose works were stylistically closest to Twachtman's was Willard Metcalf, who had studied at the

Above left: J. Alden Weir, a committed art activist, helped found both the Society of American Artists and the Ten, aided struggling colleagues, and advised collectors.

Above: Whistler's self-portrait, *Arrangement in Gray: Portrait of the Painter,* 1872.

Académie Julian and who spent the first part of his life as a successful illustrator. When he decided to turn to painting, he specialized in landscapes, especially seasonal ones. Comfortable within the limits of his style, Metcalf did not experiment as other members of the Ten did, and his work remained popular until his death in 1925.

The most unusual paintings created by a member of the Ten were those of Thomas Wilmer Dewing, who painted portraits and figure pieces. Dewing's works are mysterious, ambiguous, and somewhat disturbing. His figures are rarely connected to a real world, even when placed in a room. His idealized female figures are almost Pre-Raphaelite in his early works, but are refined and isolated in the later paintings, which borrowed from the Dutch Masters such as Jan Vermeer.

Not all of the Ten were oriented to New York. Unlike the previously mentioned artists, Frank Benson, Edmund Tarbell, and Joseph De Camp all taught in Boston during the winter, and were perhaps the most conventional painters of the group. Of the three, Benson was the most popular and was one of the best-selling artists of his day. In his lifetime he was well known for his etchings of birds in flight, but his fame today rests on his

series of portraits, mostly the young women in his family. Benson's works capture the summer atmosphere of an innocent and carefree world at a time when a number of people could afford to spend months away from the hot, un-airconditioned cities.

Like Benson, Edmund Tarbell was born in Massachusetts in 1862, and taught at the Boston Museum School. Like Benson, he painted figures and family groups, but many of his figures are closer to the mysterious, isolated women in Dewing's works than to Benson's golden daughters. Many of his interiors use the old Dutch effect of light from a single window to illuminate a figure, creating a mood of tranquillity and harmony.

The third Bostonian, Joseph De Camp, had studied in Munich with Duveneck, and used lighting effects that were similar to Tarbell's in many of his portraits. His few landscapes, which he seems to have painted for his own pleasure, are more Impressionistic in palette and brushwork. De Camp had been introduced to the work of Vermeer through a monograph probably written by Bostonian Philip Leslie Hale. Hale also taught at the Boston Museum School and was the art critic of the *Boston Herald*. Although Hale worked in the Impressionist style, and was a contemporary of Benson and Tarbell, he had not been invited to join the Ten.

The last two artists in the original group, Edward Simmons and Robert Reid, were even less in the mainstream than Dewing. Both were muralists, although Simmons was also known for his marine paintings, and Reid also painted figure pieces and landscapes. Reid occasionally used a very pale palette, and enjoyed placing his figures against a background of solid flowers or an elaborate screen. Some of his work is almost Post-

Above: *Portrait of John Twachtman* by Weir.

Below: The Benson family at Wooster Farm, 1907.

Impressionist, pointing toward future art movements of the early twentieth century. Another painter whose compositions frequently consisted of figures of women in gardens of flowers that filled the canvas was Frederick Frieseke, who remained in France. He moved to the house in Giverny next to Monet's, that had once been rented to Theodore Robinson in 1906. His paintings of women in gardens are much more like those of Renoir than Monet.

At Twachtman's death, his place in the Ten was taken by William Merritt Chase, one of the most important American artistic figures of the late nineteenth century. Born in 1849, Chase was an eclectic painter. He studied at the National Academy of Design in New York, shared a studio with Duveneck in Munich, and accompanied Duveneck and Twachtman to Paris in 1877. He returned to New York in 1878, and took a studio in the well-known artists' building on Tenth Street in New York. He taught privately and at the Art Students' League in between his many trips to Europe. In 1885 he toured Europe with Whistler, and the two artists painted portraits of one

another. When Chase married, he moved first to Brooklyn, and later to Shinnecock, Long Island. In both places he painted some of his finest landscapes – the glorious paintings of the sandy, low hills and dark waters frequently include members of Chase's rapidly growing family. Chase was flamboyant; he did not abandon the Bohemian lifestyle of the Paris ateliers, as did other painters who felt that the puritanical attitude that had governed American cultural life was only waiting for them to make a mistake. Chase brought his unconventional style back to Tenth Street, along with his pottery, oriental rugs, and screens. But Chase was not a *poseur*. He worked extremely hard, served as President of the Society of American Artists for ten years, and was responsible for mounting an exhibition of modern French painting in New York in 1883.

The American Impressionist painters were bringing their style into the mainstream of American art. However, other forces were rising. Several painters who had studied with the Impressionists, including Vonnoh's pupils Robert Henri, John Sloan, and William Glackens, had formed their own group in reaction to the sentimental turn they felt the American Impressionist movement had taken. (American Impressionism was by and large more delicate than French Impressionism, and that delicacy could, and did, turn into sentimentality.) Known as the Eight, they held their first exhibition in 1908, and featured works of urban realism that gave them their nickname The Ashcan School. Like the Impressionists, not all of them held strictly to the new style. Glackens began to work in a more Post-Impressionist style, like his friend, Maurice Prendergast. Part of this was his choice of subject matter. Like the Impressionists before them, the Eight painted the life they saw about them, but it was a lower class of life than the Impressionists witnessed. These artists sought out the playgrounds of the lower-middle class, such as Revere Beach, near Boston, which had changed with the influx of immigrants.

Maurice Prendergast, although one of the Eight, was unique in his transformation of Impressionism. On his return from Europe in the 1890s, he began a series of watercolors that used clear patches of color to create vivacious landscapes filled with simplified figures. This lightness of style, when executed in oil, was transformed to a more abstract one, in the manner of Cézanne. Prendergast was one of the painters who exhibited at the International Exhibition of Modern Art, now known as the Armory Show, in 1913. Glackens was one of the organizers, and many of the Eight were exhibitors. But the greatest share of publicity was given to the modernist paintings by Georges Bracque, Pablo Picasso, and Marcel Duchamp, whose huge Futurist expression of movement, *Nude Descending the Staircase*, was a scandalous success. Once again, the leading forces of contemporary art had moved to France. The year after the Armory Show, World War I began. The safe, glorious world portrayed by Frank Benson and William Merritt Chase, which celebrated the growth of the United States, was gone. New art movements rose and fell with remarkable speed, and the American Impressionists were soon forgotten and ignored, as the earlier American painters had been.

Almost a hundred years after the first exhibition by the Ten, their work still shines, beckoning the viewer to enter a safe world, and giving that person a brilliant vision of that world. The American Impressionist movement adapted the techniques of the French style to create a particularly native school of painting, which grew to represent stability, charm, and serenity. The subjects the American Impressionists painted were familiar to their viewers, and perhaps by seeing these familiar places and objects portrayed differently, the Americans learned to open their eyes to even more abstract art movements and ideas.

Left: William Merritt Chase with students at Shinnecock Hills, c. 1901.

Below: Maurice Prendergast's *The Mall, Central Park*, 1901.

Americans Abroad

By the 1820s, a period of study in Europe had become a recognized element of artistic training for Americans. The necessity of education abroad might have been due in part to a belief in the superiority of European culture, and an attendant concept – which continues to this day – that an educated person must see firsthand the glories of older civilizations. In the same way, very few American artists were taken seriously if they had not spent some time studying abroad.

Artists interested in the classical past and the masters of the Renaissance went to Rome and Florence, while those interested in the work of their contemporaries went to Munich, Düsseldorf, and Paris. Many painters of the Hudson River School, including Albert Bierstadt and Thomas Cole, studied abroad, and traveled to Italy and Germany often. Several of them would spend summers sketching in America, and return to their studios in Florence or Rome each winter to paint vast canvases of the White Mountains or Hudson Valley.

Artists were not the only Americans who flocked to Europe in the nineteenth century. Mark Twain's *Innocents Abroad*, published in 1869, indicates that members of the upper and upper-middle classes regularly traveled in Europe for extended periods. The Cassatts of Philadelphia brought their daughter Mary to Paris for the first time in 1851 when she was seven. James Abbott McNeill Whistler also came to Europe as a child, when his father accepted a position from the Russian government. Young Whistler was given his first drawing lessons in St. Petersburg in 1845. John Singer Sargent was born in Florence while his parents were taking the Grand Tour, and didn't set foot in his own country until he was twenty. Though these three artists spent most of their lives in Europe and always seemed more at home there, they have never been considered anything but American.

By the 1880s there was a veritable flood of young American artists, wanting to improve their techniques and to learn new ones, concentrated in Paris. Author Henry James, another well-known expatriate, wrote at this time, "when today we look for 'American Art' we find it mainly in Paris. When we find it out of Paris, we at least find a good deal of Paris in it."

Among the Americans in Paris then were Childe Hassam, Robert Vonnoh, and Willard Metcalf, all of whom attended classes at the Académie Julian, and studied with Gustave Boulanger and Jules Lefebvre. Another young American working in Paris was Theodore Robinson, who studied with Charles Carolus-Duran and Jean Léon Gérôme. A friendship with Monet, whom he met in 1887, inspired a change in Robinson's style, and he began painting in the Impressionist manner, forsaking the academic realist school and the dark tones of the Barbizon. His paintings of Giverny – which includes *Bird's Eye View: Giverny, France*, a lovely atmospheric landscape of greens and grays – were among the first Impressionistic works to be exhibited in the United States. His influence on his countrymen – especially after he returned to the United States to instruct at the Pennsylvania Academy of Arts – was considerable. Robert Vonnoh, who had introduced Impressionism to the school, had persuaded Robinson to take the position in Philadelphia. Vonnoh exhibited a number of landscapes in Boston in 1891, which he described as "a record of impressions gathered out of doors during summer holydays [sic] in France in '89 and '90. . . . " In 1889 Vonnoh had been one of the Americans exhibiting at the Exposition Universelle in Paris, which was part of the celebration of the centennial of the French Revolution. Other exhibitors included Hassam, William Merritt Chase, and Robinson.

Not all the Americans working abroad came back to the United States. Sargent moved to England in 1885, and sketched and painted portraits of his friends and fellow artists along the banks of English rivers. Mary Cassatt continued to paint portraits for traveling Americans to take home, and for her French friends. She also encouraged her brother, Louisine Havemeyer, and other American collectors to add contemporary works by American artists to their private galleries.

Other young Americans studying abroad helped to popularize the Impressionist style at home. When they returned to the United States they used their newly acquired knowledge to see their own country through Impressionist eyes, and to translate it onto canvas and paper.

John Singer Sargent

Breakfast in the Loggia
1910, oil on canvas, 20½ × 28 in.
Freer Gallery of Art,
Smithsonian Institution, Washington, D.C.
(17.182)

Overleaf:
CHILDE HASSAM

April Showers, Champs Elysees, Paris
1888, oil on canvas, 12½ × 16¾ in.
Joslyn Art Museum, Omaha, NE
(1946.30)

Right:

John Singer Sargent

Two Girls with Parasols at Fladbury
1889, oil on canvas, 29½ × 25 in.
Gift of Mrs. Francis Ormond, 1950,
The Metropolitan Museum of Art, New York, NY
(50.130.13)

Mary Cassatt

Fillette au Grand Chapeau
c. 1908, pastel on buff paper, 25¼ × 19½ in.
Henry E. Huntington Library and
Art Gallery, San Marino, CA

MARY CASSATT

Lydia at a Tapestry Loom
c. 1881, oil on canvas, 25¾ × 36¼ in.
Gift of The Whiting Foundation,
Flint Institute of Arts, Flint, MI
(67.32)

THEODORE ROBINSON
Bird's-Eye View: Giverny, France
1889, oil on canvas, 25¾ × 32 in.
Gift of George A. Hearn, 1910,
The Metropolitan Museum of Art, New York, NY
(10.64.9)

James McNeill Whistler

Nocturne: Grand Canal, Amsterdam
1883-84, watercolor on paper, 8¹⁵⁄₁₆ × 11³⁄₁₆ in.
Freer Gallery of Art,
Smithsonian Institution, Washington, D.C.
(02.161)

Overleaf:

Robert Vonnoh

In Flanders Field Where Soldiers Sleep and Poppies Grow
c. 1892, oil on canvas, 58 × 104 in.
The Butler Institute of American Art, Youngstown, OH
(919.0.114)

John H. Twachtman
Arques-la-Bataille
1885, oil on canvas, 60 × 78⅞ in.
Morris K. Jesup Fund, 1968,
The Metropolitan Museum of Art, New York, NY
(68.52)

Overleaf:

WILLARD METCALF

Gloucester Harbor
1895, oil on canvas, 26 × 28¾ in.
Gift of George D. Pratt,
Mead Art Museum,
Amherst College, Amherst, MA

JOHN SINGER SARGENT

Home Fields
1885, oil on canvas, 28¾ × 38 in.
City of Detroit Purchase,
© The Detroit Institute of Arts, Detroit, MI
(21.72)

LANDSCAPES

The earliest paintings to be identified as landscapes are probably those found in the background of early Renaissance religious works. In the seventeenth century, such painters as Claude Lorrain and the Dutch Masters had transformed it into a recognized art form. Landscape painting grew in importance throughout the following century for two reasons: because a powerful aristocracy wished to display a vision of the land that was their power base; and through the influence of such writers as Jean Jacques Rousseau, whose image of the natural world and its native inhabitants was seen in extreme and flattering contrast to the corrupt life of urban society of that time. The subsequent rise of the Romantic movement and its emphasis on the picturesque and the beauty of nature also contributed to the rising popularity of landscape painting.

In the United States, the Hudson River School celebrated the glory of the New World, unencumbered by what they perceived to be the "stain" of civilization. On vast canvases, they portrayed a heroic vision of the natural world, taking into consideration the moral and religious attitude that was prevalent in America in the early nineteenth century. As one critic of the time wrote, "what comparison is there between the garden landscapes of England and France and the noble scenery of the Hudson, or the wild witchery of some of our unpolluted lakes and streams? One is man's nature, the other – God's."

Even as critics tried to reconcile the Hudson River School with the remnants of the puritanical attitude that had been part of American thought for so long, another American art movement, Luminism, came to prominence.

Luminism has been described as "the lyrical expression of landscape under specific conditions of light and atmosphere." The general format was parallel bands of sky and water or land, with the horizon dividing the picture, executed in a smooth, finished style, and characterized by a pervading feeling of solitude and calm. This serenity is found even in the storm pictures of Martin Johnson Heade, where the sky is jet black and the land and water are illuminated by the curious yellow light that precedes a squall.

Luminism was a precursor of Impressionism. Landscape painters had gradually been choosing to portray more intimate views of the natural world. The vast canvases that characterized the Hudson River School, such as Albert Bierstadt's *The Domes of the Yosemite*, which measured 9½ by 15 feet, had lost their popularity in favor of smaller scenes. In a flight from the grandeur that had governed landscape painting, the artist now seemed to place himself at a point where the horizon was only in the middle distance.

The Impressionists brought the landscape even closer. John Twachtman's *The Waterfall* shows a small stream tumbling over rocks almost at the observer's feet. Inspired by the *plein-air* works of the French, the artists created landscapes that drew the observer into them, to enjoy the fields and hills before them, rather than to marvel at a precipice from miles away.

Those who enjoyed the camaraderie of the artists' colonies at Giverny, Barbizon, and Broadway were delighted to join similar colonies that sprang up in their own country in Gloucester, Massachusetts; Old Lyme, Connecticut; or New Hope, Pennsylvania. Instead of painting the beaches of Brittany, or the harbor at Boulogne, they turned to the dunes of Long Island, as did William Merritt Chase; or the granite coast of New Hampshire and Maine, as did Childe Hassam and Frank Benson. Just as they had previously enjoyed the mists rising over the Seine and the Oise, now they basked in the clear ocean light of America.

The Impressionists were also interested in painting an inhabited landscape, "man's nature," in fact, rather than "God's." Willard Metcalf's *The North Country*, which might have been a typical subject for a painter of the Hudson River School, shows Vermont's Mount Ascutney dominating the scene. Metcalf, unlike Hudson River School artists, has placed the village of Perkinsville in the middle distance, bringing the subject down to size. He also chose to paint it on a bright day in early spring, before the budding of the leaves, rather than in the lush summer or gloriously colored autumn so beloved of such painters as Sanford Gifford and Frederic Church. Though *The North Country* was painted in 1923, at the end of Metcalf's life when the style had fallen into disfavor, the characteristic short brush strokes and brighter palette also mark this painting as Impressionistic.

J. ALDEN WEIR

Building a Dam, Shetucket
1908, oil on canvas, 31¼ × 40¼ in.
Purchase from the J. H. Wade Fund,
The Cleveland Museum of Art, Cleveland, OH
(27.171)

William Merritt Chase

Landscape: Shinnecock, Long Island
n. d., oil on wood panel, 14½ × 16 in.
Gift of Prof. Francis A. Comstock, Class of 1919,
The Art Museum,
Princeton University , Princeton, NJ
(39-35)

WILLARD METCALF

The North Country
1923, oil on canvas, 40 × 45¼ in.
George A. Hearn Fund,
The Metropolitan Museum of Art, New York, NY
(24.60)

THEODORE ROBINSON
Road By the Mill
1892, oil on canvas, 20 × 25 in.
Gift of Alfred T. and Eugenia I. Goshorn,
The Cincinnati Art Museum, Cincinnati, OH
(1924.70)

John Singer Sargent

A Backwater, Calcot Mill Near Reading
1888, oil on canvas, 20³⁄₁₆ × 27 in.
Gift of J. Gilman D'Arcy Paul,
The Baltimore Museum of Art, Baltimore, MD
(1968.22)

JOHN TWACHTMAN
Gloucester Harbor
1901, oil on canvas, 25 × 25 in.
*Collection of the Canajoharie Library and Art Gallery, Canajoharie
NY*

Overleaf:

EDWARD POTTHAST

At the Beach
n. d., oil on board, 5 × 7 in.
*The Warner Collection of Gulf States Paper Corporation,
Tuscaloosa, AL*

JOHN TWACHTMAN

The Waterfall
c. 1890-1900, oil on canvas, 30 × 30¼ in.
Worcester Art Museum, Worcester, MA
(1907.91)

EDWARD SIMMONS

Boston Public Gardens
1893, oil on canvas, 18×26 in.
© *Daniel J. Terra Collection,*
Terra Museum of American Art, Chicago, IL
(34.1984)

Overleaf:

CHILDE HASSAM

Coast Scene, Isles of Shoals
1901, oil on canvas, 24⅞×30⅛ in.
Gift of George A. Hearn, 1909,
The Metropolitan Museum of Art, New York, NY
(09.72.6)

BUILDINGS AND BRIDGES

The American Impressionists, like their French counterparts, were eager to explore new subjects such as cityscapes. This choice of subject matter was another point of division between the French artistic establishment and the Impressionists. The artistic establishment believed that a picturesque peasant cottage was a suitable subject, but a Parisian streetcorner was not. When Edgar Degas chose to paint the world around him, he painted the demimondaines in the Paris cafes and the dancers backstage at the ballet. When Pierre-Auguste Renoir and Claude Monet painted the gaiety at *La Grenouillère*, the critics were aware of and appalled by the reputation of the restaurant and were shocked by the execution of the paintings that depicted it. A classical nude was permissible; Edouard Manet's *Olympia* was not. The Impressionists believed that anything found in their world was a suitable subject to portray, even those aspects of life that some people would prefer to remain hidden.

This bold outlook was an impetus to the Americans. In their own country, where the artistic establishment was less entrenched, and where the very lack of artistic conventions gave them a freedom unknown in the Europe, American painters could choose to immortalize any aspect of their country.

The late nineteenth century was the era of expansion in the United States. The growth of the cities after the Civil War, stimulated by industry and the growing tide of immigration, was seen as a sign of progress. But in choosing to paint their growing cities, the American Impressionists turned away from the more sordid aspects of urban life. The city scenes they painted reflected the characteristic optimism of the nation. A sense of comfort and affluence permeates Childe Hassam's paintings of the squares of brownstones and the new triumphal arch at Washington Square. They show aspects of the New York of Edith Wharton and Henry James. Hassam also captured the changing aspects of New York in the early years of the new century when the first skyscrapers were being built. Other painters chose to paint the city at night, perhaps influenced by the nocturnes of Whistler.

It was not just the urban scenes that caught the attention of the Impressionists. Any building under the right conditions might become a subject. In several paintings by J. Alden Weir, New England mill towns are given the grace of French villages; no negative aspects of industrialization are portrayed. *The Little Hotel* by Joseph De Camp resembles one on the Seine. The proportions and the green shutters on a nearby house give the observer a clue that the painting was done in New England.

In contrast to the painters of the Hudson River School, the Impressionists delighted in painting all kinds of man-made structures, including bridges. This may have been due in part to their appreciation of the way light plays over a bridge, especially with regard to the bridge's reflection and the way light is reflected off the water. This can be seen very clearly in Weir's *The Red Bridge*, which is also an example of the Japanese influence on painters of the period. Hassam's painting of the Columbian Exposition has a similar oriental feeling.

Bridges were also used by the Impressionists to create a point of focus within an otherwise flat landscape. They also found the people on a bridge would create an interesting composition. The different materials that are used in bridge building also gave the Impressionists interesting patterns of color, shadow, and light to paint. John Twachtman even built his own bridge across Horseneck Brook on his property in Greenwich, Connecticut, which he portrayed on canvas several times using the strong vertical of the wooden piers in pleasing contrast to the natural surroundings.

Left:

Theodore Robinson

Union Square in Winter
1895, oil on canvas, 20×17 in.
Gift of A. W. Stanley Estate,
New Britain Museum of American Art,
New Britain, CT

Childe Hassam

Union Square in Spring
1896, oil on canvas, 21½×21½ in.
Smith College Museum of Art,
Northampton, MA

CHILDE HASSAM

Bridge at Old Lyme
1908, oil on canvas, 24×27 in.
Eva Underhill Holbrook Memorial Collection of American Art,
Gift of Alfred T. Holbrook,
Georgia Museum of Art,
The University of Georgia, Athens, GA
(45.47)

JOSEPH DE CAMP
The Little Hotel
1903, oil on canvas, 20 × 24¹⁄₁₆ in.
Joseph E. Temple Fund,
The Pennsylvania Academy of the Fine Arts, Philadelphia, PA
(1904.2)

65

WILLARD METCALF

May Night
1907, oil on canvas, 39½ × 38⅜ in.
Museum Purchase, Gallery Fund,
Collection of the Corcoran Gallery of Art, Washington, D.C.
(7.7)

Right:

J. ALDEN WEIR

The Fishing Party
1915, oil on canvas, 28 × 23⅛ in.
© *The Phillips Collection, Washington, D.C.*
(2072)

J. Alden Weir

The Red Bridge
1895, oil on canvas, 24¼ × 33¾ in.
Gift of George A. Hearn, 1910,
The Metropolitan Museum of Art, New York, NY
(10.64.9)

EDWARD REDFIELD

New Hope
1927, oil on canvas, 50⅛ × 56⅛ in.
Joseph E. Temple Fund,
The Pennsylvania Academy of the Fine Arts, Philadelphia, PA
(1927.7)

Theodore Robinson

La Débâcle
1892, oil on canvas, 18×22 in.
Gift of General and Mrs. Edward Clinton Young,
Lang Art Gallery,
Scripps College, Claremont, CA

71

Left:

JOHN TWACHTMAN

The White Bridge
1900, oil on canvas, 30¼ × 25⅛ in.
Gift of Emily Sibley Watson,
Memorial Art Gallery of the University of Rochester,
Rochester, NY
(16.9)

ARTHUR CLIFTON GOODWIN

On South Boston Pier
1904, oil on canvas, 15⅞ × 20 in.
Gift of Florence Scott Libbey,
The Toledo Museum of Art, Toledo, OH
(1950.307)

GUY C. WIGGINS

Metropolitan Tower
1912, oil on canvas, 34 1/16 × 40 1/8 in.
George A. Hearn Fund,
The Metropolitan Museum of Art, New York, NY
(12.105.4)

J. ALDEN WEIR
The Plaza: Nocturne
1911, oil on canvas mounted on wood, 29 × 39½ in.
Gift of Joseph H. Hirshhorn, 1966,
Hirshhorn Museum and Sculpture Garden,
Smithsonian Institution, Washington, D.C.
(66.5508)

CHILDE HASSAM

Columbian Exposition, Chicago
1892, gouache en grisaille on paper, 10¼×14 in.
© *Daniel J. Terra Collection,*
Terra Museum of American Art, Chicago, IL
(15.1980)

PORTRAITS AND CHARACTER STUDIES

The earliest works by American painters had been portraits. The more sophisticated eighteenth-century painters such as Benjamin West, John Singleton Copley, and the Peales followed the conventions of such English court painters as Thomas Gainsborough, Thomas Lawrence, and Joshua Reynolds, who placed their elaborately dressed, usually aristocratic sitters in a classical setting or stylized garden. At the same time, self-taught, itinerant painters such as Robert Feke, Ammi Phillips, and Edward Hicks, whose style is now described as primitive or folk, usually painted ordinary people against indistinct backgrounds or humble interiors. But the desire to preserve a person's features knew no social boundary.

In the years following the Civil War, which saw the establishment of a number of great American fortunes and the rise of the robber barons, family portraits, especially those painted by a society painter, became a necessary possession for a person of culture and discernment. John Singer Sargent, who may be best known for his series of remarkable portraits, very often followed the conventions set up by the great portraitists of the past and painted his sitters in evening clothes, with the women in their finest jewels. But some of Sargent's most successful portraits are the less elaborate ones. He painted Mr. and Mrs. Isaac Newton Phelps Stokes in everyday clothes, and the only visible jewelry was Mrs. Stokes's wedding and engagement rings and her cut steel belt buckle. Sargent painted Robert Louis Stevenson several times. One portrait shows the author in a wicker chair, his legs crossed informally, and a cigarette in one slender and beautifully modeled hand. Whistler was another painter renowned for his portraits, and was painstaking in their execution. He would often require his models to pose for hours, and then scrape down the entire figure and begin again to obtain the appearance of delicacy and grace which was the hallmark of his work.

The Impressionists' paintings of people in unguarded moments against a backdrop of informal interiors have become valuable records of life in the late nineteenth century. One of the most charming of these is Lillian Westcott Hale's Zeffy in Bed. Rose Zeffler, a model used by both Hale and her husband Philip, is shown barely awake, her face is the only clearly defined part of the work, which is suffused with a beautifully soft light.

Many artists also used their families as models, and as integral parts of paintings that were more than simple portraits. The dark-haired figure in William Merritt Chase's A Friendly Call is his wife Alice, whom he painted often. The composition, which reveals a great deal about the life of the painter, portrays an extraordinary tension between the two figures, and suggests that despite its title, the call is not so friendly.

The informality that was becoming part of life was frequently best observed in the various places that attracted artists during the summer. Frank Benson painted his children again and again on the headlands and in their garden on the island of North Haven in Maine's Penobscot Bay. In his paintings they become the very image of golden youth and happy childhood, although they are always recognizable. Chase also painted his children, especially his oldest daughter, in many of his compositions – including the Shinnecock landscapes.

At the other extreme are the paintings of Thomas Dewing, who by putting his figures against indefinite backgrounds created a general feeling of isolation and disquiet, which is far removed from the usual tranquil and comfortable life seen in most Impressionist paintings.

Left:

JOHN SINGER SARGENT

Mr. and Mrs. Isaac Newton Phelps Stokes
1897, oil on canvas, 85¼ × 39¾ in.
*Bequest of Edith Minturn Phelps Stokes (Mrs. I. N.), 1938,
The Metropolitan Museum of Art, New York, NY*
(38.104)

WILLIAM MERRITT CHASE

"Did You Speak to Me?"
1900, oil on canvas, 38×41 in.
The Butler Institute of American Art, Youngstown, OH
(959.0.106)

Right:

JOSEPH DE CAMP

The Seamstress
1916, oil on canvas, 36¼×28 in.
Museum Purchase,
The Corcoran Gallery of Art, Washington, D.C.
(16.4)

Left:

Lillian Wescott Hale

Zeffy in Bed
1912, oil on canvas, 30 × 21¾ in.
NAA-Beatrice D. Rohman Fund,
Sheldon Memorial Art Gallery,
University of Nebraska, Lincoln, NE
1974. (N-329)

Frank Benson

Girl Playing Solitaire
1909, oil on canvas, 50½ × 40½ in.
Worcester Art Museum, Worcester, MA
(1909.14)

THOMAS DEWING
Girl with Lute
n. d., oil on wood panel, 24×17¾ in.
Freer Gallery of Art,
Smithsonian Institution, Washington, D.C.
(5.2)

JAMES MCNEILL WHISTLER

**Purple and Rose: The Lange
Leizen of the Six Marks**
1864, oil on canvas, 36 × 24¼ in.
*John G. Johnson Collection,
Philadelphia Museum of Art, Philadelphia, PA
(J.1112)*

Left:

Edmund Tarbell

Woman in Pink and Green
1897, oil on canvas, 48 × 36⅛ in.
Collection of Mr. and Mrs. Raymond J. Horowitz,
The Metropolitan Museum of Art, New York, NY
(L.1982.119)

Thomas Dewing

The Necklace
1907, oil on wood, 20 × 15¾ in.
Gift of John Gellatly,
National Museum of American Art,
Smithsonian Institution, Washington, D.C.
(Courtesy, Art Resource, NY)
(1929.6.40)

WILLIAM MERRITT CHASE
A Friendly Call
1895, oil on canvas, 30⅛ × 48¼ in.
Chester Dale Collection,
National Gallery of Art, Washington, D.C.
(1943.1.2)

JOHN SINGER SARGENT

Robert Louis Stevenson
1887, oil on canvas, 20¹⁄₁₆ × 24⁵⁄₁₆ in.
Bequest of Mr. and Mrs. Charles Phelps Taft,
The Taft Museum, Cincinnati, OH
(1931.472)

Right:

WILLIAM MERRITT CHASE

Portrait of Miss E. (Portrait of Lydia Field Emmet)
1892, oil on canvas, 71⅞ × 36¼ in.
Gift of the Artist,
The Brooklyn Museum, Brooklyn, NY
(15.316)

GARDENS

It may have been the colors that first attracted the Impressionists to the garden as a subject. The bold colors of many flowers, their chance juxtaposition, and their intensity under full sun provided the artists with a perfect composition wherever they turned. The contrast of light and shadow and the dappling effect of leaves also appealed to many of the Impressionists.

The garden was a new subject. Previously they had been painted only as minor aspects of house or estate portraits. As the Impressionists began to take a more intimate view of life around them, they found the garden was another part of life to enjoy. There was a great surge of enthusiasm for gardens and gardening in the 1880s, especially in England and the United States, and a concurrent interest in paintings of gardens.

Many of the Impressionists had painted formal gardens, in Italy, but these had been studies in the contrast between the dark green of ornamental hedges and trees and the golden stones used for fountains and statuary. The gardening revival had created interest in two distinct types of gardens. One was the wild garden, in which wild flowers and bulbs were planted seemingly at random, in fields and woods, and allowed to naturalize. The other was the old-fashioned garden, planted with such hardy perennials and biennials as poppies, phlox, and hollyhocks. Since many of these artists spent their summers in art colonies such as Old Lyme, Connecticut — which had been a thriving seaport until the railroad and steam ships had taken over the coastal shipping trade — they became aware of gardens and houses where time had, to a certain extent, stood still.

The last decades of the nineteenth century and the first few years of the twentieth were also the years of the arts and crafts movement and the colonial revival. Both movements sought to return to a simpler way of life, and created an atmosphere of appreciation for the nation's past and all aspects of colonial culture.

The painters who studied in France, especially those who had lived and worked at Giverny, were aware of how well the informal garden suited them as a subject. The ancient fields of France, which were filled in season with wild poppies, became the subject of many paintings, including those by Robert Vonnoh. Those who created wild gardens were hoping for just that effect, with the wild poppies providing a natural color accent. Another artist who continued to work in France was Frederick Frieseke, who said he knew nothing about horticulture. "If you are looking at a mass of flowers in sunlight out of doors you see a sparkle of spots of different colors: I paint them that way." By concentrating on the shape and color of flowers in full sunlight, he managed to produce recognizable blooms in many of his paintings.

Those who returned to the United States used their knowledge gained in Europe to paint American gardens filled with American plants under American skies. One of these was Childe Hassam, who spent some of his summers on the Isles of Shoals, staying at the hotel run by the well-known horticulturist and poet Celia Thaxter. Hassam painted Thaxter's garden over and over again, enjoying the "most breathtaking riot of color," as Thaxter described it in her book, *An Island Garden*, which was illustrated by Hassam. After Thaxter's death in 1894, Hassam worked in Old Lyme and Cos Cob, Connecticut, before he finally settled in Easthampton. In all three places he painted gardens, enjoying the contrast of bright flowers and weathered clapboards, which can be seen in *Old House and Garden, East Hampton* [sic].

Another member of the Ten, John Twachtman, became famous for the paintings of his house and garden in Greenwich, Connecticut. Twachtman painted all aspects of his garden, including the vegetables, the flowering shrubs, and the potted plants in the greenhouse. It may be that in the paintings of gardens, caught in the golden light of summer, the American Impressionists reached the zenith of their art.

Left:

FREDERICK FRIESEKE

Lady in a Garden
1912, oil on canvas, 31⅞ × 25¾ in.
© *Daniel J. Terra Collection,*
Terra Museum of American Art, Chicago, IL
(1.1982)

Overleaf:

WILLIAM MERRITT CHASE

Prospect Park, Brooklyn
n. d., oil on canvas, 17⅜ × 22⅜ in.
Gift of the Misses Adeline F. and Caroline R. Wing,
Colby College Museum of Art, Waterville, ME

EDWARD WILBUR DEAN HAMILTON

Summer at Campobello, New Brunswick
c. 1890-1900, oil on canvas, 28 × 28 in.
Bequest of Maxim Karolik,
Courtesy, Museum of Fine Arts, Boston, MA
(64.463)

WILLIAM CHADWICK

On the Porch
1908, oil on canvas, 24 × 30 in.
Gift of Elizabeth Chadwick O'Connell,
Florence Griswold Museum, Old Lyme, CT

JOHN SINGER SARGENT
The Luxembourg Gardens at Twilight
1879, oil on canvas, 29 × 36½ in.
Gift of the Martin B. Koon Memorial Collection,
The Minneapolis Institute of Arts, Minneapolis, MN
(16.20)

Philip Leslie Hale

The Crimson Rambler
1909, oil on canvas, 25¼ × 30³⁄₁₆ in.
Joseph E. Temple Fund,
The Pennsylvania Academy of the Fine Arts, Philadelphia, PA
(1909.12)

GARI MELCHERS

The Unpretentious Garden
c. 1903-09, oil on canvas, 33¾ × 40¼ in.
Museum Purchase,
Telfair Academy of Arts and Sciences, Savannah, GA
(1917.2)

Right:

CHILDE HASSAM

Old House and Garden, East Hampton, Long Island
1898, oil on canvas, 24¹⁄₁₆ × 20 in.
Horace C. Henry Collection,
Henry Art Gallery,
University of Washington, Seattle, WA
(26.70)

Left:

CHILDE HASSAM

Gathering Flowers in a French Garden
1888, oil on canvas, 28 × 21⅝ in.
Theodore T. and Mary G. Ellis Collection,
Worcester Art Museum, Worcester, MA
(1940.87)

JOHN TWACHTMAN

Azaleas
1898, oil on canvas, 30 × 24 in.
Maier Museum of Art,
Randolph-Macon Woman's College, Lynchburg, VA

CHILDE HASSAM

Spring, The Dogwood Tree
1921, oil on canvas, 43 × 46 in.
Gift of the Benwood Foundation,
Hunter Museum of Art, Chattanooga, TN
(HMA76.3)

ROBERT REID
Fleur-de-Lis
1899, oil on canvas, 44⅛ × 42¾ in.
Gift of George A. Hearn, 1907,
The Metropolitan Museum of Art, New York, NY
(07.140)

EDMUND TARBELL

Three Sisters: A Study in June Sunlight
1890, oil on canvas, 35⅛ × 40⅛
Gift of Mrs. Montgomery, Sears,
Milwaukee Art Museum, Milwaukee, WI
(1925.1)

Poppies
1888, oil on canvas, 13×18 in.
*James E. Roberts Fund,
Indianapolis Museum of Art,
Indianapolis, IN*
(71.8)

LIST OF COLOR PLATES

Picture Credits
Archives of American Art, Smithsonian Institution, Washington, D.C.: 12, 16.
Cincinnati Art Museum, OH: 15(top).
Essex Institute, Salem, MA: 15(bottom).
Florence Griswold Museum, Old Lyme, CT: 6.
The Historical Society of the Town of Greenwich, CT: 10.
National Museum of American Art, Smithsonian Institution, Washington, D.C.: 14(top left).
National Portrait Gallery, Smithsonian Institution, Washington, D.C.: 13.
Terra Museum of American Art, Chicago, IL, Gift of Mr. Ira Spanierman, 1985: 11(top).

Acknowledgments
The publisher would like to thank the following people who helped in the preparation of this book: Don Longabucco, the designer; Susan Bernstein, the editor; and Sara Dunphy, the picture editor.

Artwork
PAGE 7: WINSLOW HOMER
Sunlight and Shadow
1872, oil on canvas, 15¾×22½ in.
Gift of Charles Savage Homer
Cooper-Hewitt Museum, The Smithsonian Institution's National Museum of Design, New York, NY
(1917-14-7)

PAGE 8: MARY CASSATT
Woman with a Pearl Necklace in a Loge
1879, oil on canvas, 31⅝×23 in.
Bequest of Charlotte Dorrance Wright
Philadelphia Museum of Art, PA
(1978-1-5)

PAGE 9: JAMES MCNEILL WHISTLER
The Princess from the Land of Porcelain
1864, oil on canvas, 79⁹⁄₁₀×46⅔ in.
Freer Gallery of Art, Smithsonian Institution, Washington, D.C.

PAGE 11: THEODORE ROBINSON
Two in a Boat
1891, oil on cardboard, 9¼×13⅝ in.
The Phillips Collection, Washington, D.C.
(1641)

PAGE 14: JAMES MCNEILL WHISTLER
Arrangement in Gray: Portrait of the Painter
1872, oil on canvas, 29½×21 in.
Bequest of Henry Glover Stevens in memory of Ellen P. Stevens and Mary M. Stevens
© *The Detroit Institute of Arts, MI*
(34.27)

PAGE 17: MAURICE PRENDERGAST
The Mall, Central Park
1901, watercolor, 13⅞×19¾ in.
© *1988 The Art Institute of Chicago.*
All Rights Reserved.
The Olivia Shaler Swan Memorial Collection.
(1939.431)